JOE MONTANA ★ JERRY RICE

JOE MONTANA ★ JERRY RICE

RICHARD J. BRENNER

EAST END PUBLISHING
New York

To Jason, Halle and Anita, with great love and thanks. And to the many wonderful people who have helped me along the way.

JOE MONTANA * JERRY RICE

ISBN: 0-943403-05-7

First Printing / July 1990

Cover Photos: Jerry Rice front and back cover by Michael Zagaris. Joe Montana front cover by Louis A. Raynor, SportsChrome East/West. Joe Montana back cover by Mitchell B. Reibel, SportsChrome East/West. All inside photos by Michael Zagaris.

This book is published by East End Publishing, 54 Alexander Drive, Syosett, NY 11791.

Printed in the United States of America

0 9 8 7 6 5 4 3 2 1

Bibliography

Sports Illustrated
Sport Magazine
Time Magazine
People Magazine
The Sporting News
Newsweek magazine
*Dan Marino*Joe Montana,* by John Holmstrom, published by Avon Books, 1985.
Audibles: My Life in Football, by Joe Montana and Bob Raissman, Published by Wm. Morrow Co., 1986.

Contents

JOE MONTANA

1

The Natural

Joe Montana was born June 11, 1956, in New Eagle, Pennsylvania, and was raised in Monongahela, a working-class community about thirty miles upriver from Pittsburgh.

That area of Western Pennsylvania has produced an unusual amount of great quarterbacks, including Dan Marino and NFL Hall-of-Famers George Blanda, John Unitas, and Joe Namath.

And although no one could have guessed back in 1956 that Joe would one day grow up to become the greatest of them all, he did show signs that he might be an exceptional athlete at an early age. "Sometimes you just look at a kid and know he's a natural," remembers his father, also named Joe. "I'd come home from work at lunchtime. He was about seven or eight years old. He'd have a ball and a bat in his hands, standing there, waiting for me when I came in the door."

Joe Sr., who worked as a manager in a finance company along with his wife, Theresa, who was a secretary in the same office, always made time to toss a ball around or help little Joe practice. What impressed Joe Sr., who was a pretty good athlete himself, was his son's enthusiasm as much as his natural abilities. Joe just loved to play ball.

Joe joined his first organized football team, the Monongahela Little Wildcats, when he was only eight years old. While he played a lot of positions on the baseball diamond, when he played football, he was always the quarterback. Even in backyard practices Joe Sr. would run the pass patterns while Joe would fade back and try to spin tight spirals to his dad.

Joe was enrolled in organized sports programs on a year-round basis. His uniform changings between football, basketball, and baseball were as regular as the calendar. Joe loved playing all three sports, but especially basketball. "Because everyone on the court has total involvement," says Joe. "It's like tag. You have to be moving all the time. I loved dodging, faking, and feinting."

Joe even loved practicing at first, but then one day, when he was ten years old, Joe felt burnt out from constantly playing ball. He thought he might like to get involved in some non-sports activity, such as the Boy Scouts. So he told his dad that he wanted to quit the football team. The news hit Joe Sr. like a slap in the face. He had put a lot of his energy and his own dreams into Joe's boyhood games, and he was reluctant to have it all come to a sudden stop. Joe was told that he would have to wait until after the season was finished. "I don't want you to ever quit anything you've started," insisted his father. So Joe finished out the season and never did quit playing football. And while the world lost a tenderfoot, it gained a great quarterback.

Joe won the starting-quarterback spot during his sophomore year at Ringgold High. It was there, under the guidance of head coach Chuck Abramski and quarterback coach Jeff Petrucco, that Joe began to develop the talent and the style that would soon lead him out of Monongahela. The Ringgold offense was based on a mobile quarterback who could throw on the run, and that ability would prove invaluable to Joe throughout his career.

By the time Joe was in his junior year, the college coaches were competing for his attention. For a while, Joe, an all-state hoopster, seriously considered attending North Carolina State on a basketball scholarship. But even then Joe dreamed of becoming a professional athlete, and he didn't think his talent would let him soar to that level on a basketball court. And while some people thought that Joe had the talent to become a major league shortstop, when it came time to make the final decision, Joe decided to accept a football scholarship to attend the University of Notre Dame. It was a decision that brought a smile to the face of his dad, who had always hoped that Joe would play for the Fighting Irish.

Notre Dame has the richest football tradition of any college in the country. Like the Los Angeles Lakers and the Boston Celtics in professional basketball, Notre Dame's program stands for excellence on the gridiron.

2

The Comeback Kid

Joe had been a hotshot high-school all-American, but at Notre Dame he was only one of *seven* freshman quarterbacks. During Joe's first year, he never even got to practice Notre Dame's plays. He was the quarterback for the "scout team," the squad that acts out the offensive plays of the varsity's next opponent. On a football team, the scout squad is one rank above the tackling dummies.

Joe had always been the star, the main attraction, but at ND it was almost as if he didn't exist. And adding to Joe's football woes was the fact that he was away from home, alone for the first time in his young life and suffering from homesickness. But luckily for Joe, he was able to draw on his self-confidence to see him through those uncertain times. "The key was that I've always believed I could walk onto a football field and make things happen. No matter how many people said I couldn't, I knew I could."

Joe finally got his chance to strut his stuff in the third game of his sophomore season, after the starter got knocked senseless. Joe threw his first college touchdown pass and scored a TD himself while leading Notre Dame to a 31–7 win over Northwestern. But the following Saturday, Joe was back on the bench, collecting splinters.

Joe's next opportunity came two weeks later, when coach Dan Devine sent him into an almost hopeless situation. With the game deep in the fourth quarter, the Irish trailed North Carolina, who were playing at home, 14–6. The Tar Heels' blue-jerseyed fans were whooping it up in the stands while the Notre Dame players were sucking up oxygen in the 90°weather.

But Joe, taking advantage even of that slight opportunity, quickly took the Irish 73 yards for the score and then connected on a two-point pass conversion to tie the score. Notre Dame got the ball back with just over a minute to play, 80 yards away from the North Carolina end zone. Devine sent in a running play, but Joe, using his football instincts, changed the call to a pass play at the line of scrimmage. Joe delivered the ball; the defender missed the tackle, and the receiver did the rest, going all the way in for the score that gave ND a thrilling win. Moose Krause, their athletic director, was ecstatic. "I've been around since the days of Knute Rockne," he said, using the name of the Irish' most famous coach, "and I'm telling you, this was the greatest comeback by a Notre Dame team I've ever seen."

Although no one could have guessed it at the time, the North Carolina game was only the first of many down-to-the-wire finishes that would earn Joe the nickname of "The Comeback Kid." But despite Joe's late-game heroics, stardom did not come quickly. Joe finished his sophomore season on the bench, where he had begun it, and then he was forced to sit out the following year when he suffered a shoulder injury in a preseason practice.

When Joe returned for his third season, he was the third-string quarterback, warming the bench yet again. In the team's third game, Joe watched as Devine yanked the starting quarterback. And even after the second stringer went out with a serious injury, the coach ignored Joe and sent the starter back into the game. It was the lowest time in Joe's college career. "At that point, I felt totally beaten."

But then, with less than two minutes left in the third quarter and ND trailing Purdue 24–12, Devine, in desperation, sent Joe into the game. And all the Comeback Kid did was to lead the Irish on three fourth-quarter scoring drives, including the game winner with only 1:39 left to play. Joe kept the starting job and ND kept winning, including a blowout win over the

University of Texas in the Cotton Bowl. The 38–10 win over the Longhorns, who went into the game as the number-one college football team in the country, established the Irish as national collegiate champions.

The following year, Joe's senior season, Notre Dame returned to the Cotton Bowl to face the University of Houston. And in his final college game, the Miracle Man led the Irish to the greatest comeback in college football history.

The weather that day was more Alaskan than Texan. An ice storm had hammered the city, and the winds whipping through the nearly deserted stadium created a wind-chill factor cold enough to send a polar bear into hibernation.

Notre Dame moved ahead 12–0 in the first quarter when it had the howling wind at its back. Houston, though, used the weather in the second quarter to take a 20–12 halftime lead. But by that time Joe was shaking uncontrollably, as his body temperature had dipped to 96° and his fingers were stiff with frostbite.

While Joe sat in the locker room, covered with blankets and swallowing hot soup, the Cougars looked to ice the game as they increased their lead to 34–12. And though Joe reentered the game at the end of the third quarter, the situation seemed all but hopeless as Houston held on to its 22-point lead with less than eight minutes left in the game. Even after Joe and his teammates scored two TD's and added two two-point conversions, they still trailed the Cougars 34–28 with only 28 seconds left to play. With only two ticks left on the clock, the Comeback Kid took the final snap of his college career. Joe, sensing an all-out rush, rolled right and then threaded a pass into the end zone for the tying touchdown. When the extra point was good, Notre Dame had pulled out the most improbable of victories and Joe had closed out his college career with the greatest comeback of any year.

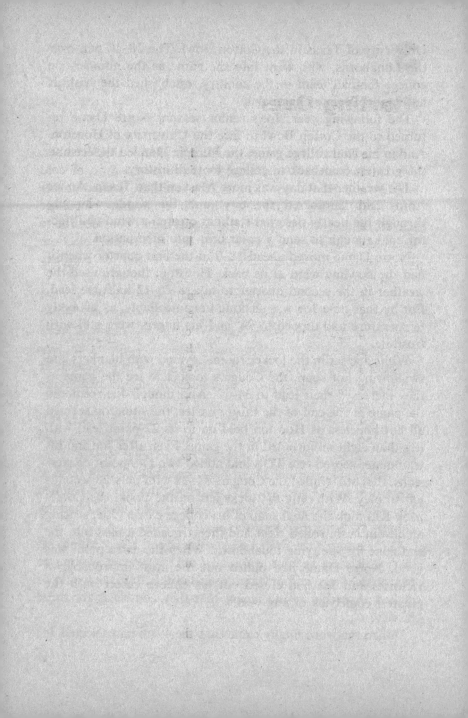

3

Starting Over

After the Cotton Bowl, Joe, who had graduated in December, decided that he had had enough of life in the land of cold winters and moved to Los Angeles while he waited to see which NFL team would select him in their draft of college players, and in which round. Pro scouts didn't consider Joe to be a "blue chip" choice, or even a late first-round selection. Their reports questioned his arm strength and his accuracy and consistency as a passer.

One of the teams that did show some interest in Joe was the San Francisco 49ers. Newly appointed head coach Bill Walsh and his quarterback coach, Sam Wyche, came down to work out Joe and a UCLA running back, James Owens. At first Joe thought that the 49ers had just asked him along because he was in the area. But as the workout continued, Joe could sense the increasing interest of Walsh and Wyche.

Joe got another boost with Walsh when he made a favorable impression on John Brodie, an ex-49er quarterback, at a Hall of Fame dinner. "Quarterbacks are funny," said Brodie. "You can usually tell as much about them from talking with them as any other way. I just saw an awareness, the way he handled himself. The next time I saw Bill Walsh, I told him if I had my choice, I'd draft that Montana guy."

On the day of the draft, Joe and his agent, Larry Muno, sat in a California beach-town restaurant, nervously waiting to hear which team and in which round of the draft Joe would be picked. A higher round meant that they could ask for more money.

When the word finally came that the 49ers had selected Joe

19

in the third round, making him the 82nd player selected in the 1979 NFL draft, Joe was relieved. He had taken a giant step toward his dream of becoming a pro football player. And since he never wanted to shovel another pile of snow, Joe was happy to have been chosen by a West Coast team. But contract talks between Joe and the 49ers became a little tense, and for a short while it looked as though Joe was going to be traded to the Denver Broncos before he ever had a chance to put on a 49ers' uniform.

Eventually the contract matters were resolved and Joe reported to his first NFL training camp, feeling tense and somewhat intimidated. Once again, Joe was starting at the end of a long line of quarterbacks. He realized that he couldn't afford to make too many mistakes or the 49ers would drop him like a hot potato. Luckily for Joe, he didn't make a lot of mistakes, and he did make a good friend in fellow rookie Dwight Clark. Clark, a tenth-round draft choice, also felt as though he was walking a very thin line, and having someone to discuss their insecurities with made it easier for both of them.

The San Francisco team that Joe was joining was a sad-sack collection that had spent a lot of years at the bottom of the NFL standings. But Bill Walsh, the new head coach, had brought a new attitude to the team and a plan to build a winner in the City by the Bay.

Part of the plan was to bring Joe along slowly so that he wouldn't have to take a constant pounding behind the 49ers' porous line. Walsh, who had developed two top quarterbacks, Dan Fouts and Ken Anderson, when he had been an assistant coach with the San Diego Chargers and Cincinnati Bengals, knew all about the care and feeding of young quarterbacks. Walsh realized that if he rushed Joe into action behind the 49ers' weak line, Joe might suffer an injury or develop a crack in his confidence. And as competitive as Joe was, he saw the wisdom to Walsh's plan. "I wanted to play my rookie season, but I came to realize that I would have been torn apart if I had played."

Most of Joe's playing time during that first year was spent as the holder on PAT's and field goals, a job that Joe considers to be among the worst in all of sports. But the 49ers, who finished with a league-worst 2–14 record, were so bad that Joe didn't have to kneel down too often.

Joe's time on the bench was made a lot easier because two veterans, O.J. Simpson, a future Hall of Fame running back who was limping his way through his last season, and Cedrick Hardman, a hard-charging defensive end, went out of their way to put his mind at ease. They explained that if he approached his role positively and worked hard to learn the system, his time would come. "Man, things aren't going to happen for you overnight," said Hardman. "Let me tell you this. I've been around and I can see you have what it takes. One day you are going to run this team. You'll get the chance, hang in." In that long season of doubt and insecurity, Hardman's words were like a life jacket in a stormy sea.

In 1980, Joe's second season, he was still playing back-up to veteran Steve DeBerg, but instead of just sulking on the bench, he was soaking up all the knowledge that he could cram into his head. He was learning how to run Walsh's complicated offense, and he was learning how to "read" the 49ers' receivers so that he'd know the routes they liked to run and the moves they made against certain defensive alignments. And Joe was also learning to understand the way pro defenses worked. "It was a crash course in sharpening my instincts," says Joe.

And while Joe was putting it all together, in his head, Walsh was giving him more time in the huddle. Joe got the starting call from Walsh in seven of the 49ers' final ten games, and the 49ers improved their record to 6–10. One of those wins, a late-season cliffhanger against the New Orleans Saints, still ranks as the greatest comeback performance in NFL history. The 49ers trailed the Saints 35–7 at halftime, and it seemed as though it was time to play Taps. But Joe, passing for 258 yards in the second half, rallied the 49ers back to life and a 38–35 overtime win. Joe had shown the NFL that he was still the Comeback Kid.

4

Number One

The way Walsh shuffled his two quarterbacks made it difficult for both Joe and DeBerg. "It was tough," said Joe. "Steve and I roomed together on the road, and after we checked into a hotel we'd head right down to the game room. We'd try to beat each other at anything. Being a quarterback means you want to be on top."

Walsh, sensing that he had to make a decisive move, traded DeBerg before the 1981 season got started. Walsh had decided that Joe was the quarterback to take the 49ers to the next level, and he was sharp enough to realize that Joe would develop more quickly if he wasn't constantly looking over his shoulder. Walsh's strategy produced immediate dividends, according to Joe. "My confidence soared when Steve was traded."

Walsh also oversaw a major overhaul of the defensive unit, starting with the college draft. He brought in three rookie defensive backs, including number-one pick Ronnie Lott, to replace a unit that had had more holes than a leaky roof. The three newcomers joined third-year player Dwight Hicks, and the hardhitting quartet quickly earned the nickname of "Dwight Hicks and the Hot Licks." Then Walsh traded for veteran middle-linebacker Jack "Hacksaw" Reynolds and Fred Dean, a sack machine of a defensive end, and the unit was primed and ready to roar.

On offense, the line, which had had more cracks than a faulty foundation the previous two years as it learned to play as a unit, was starting to come together. About the only area of weakness that the 49ers had was at the running-back position. And of course the jury was still out on their third-year quarterback, Joe Montana.

But for all the new players and the new air of confidence that seemed to suffuse the team, the 49ers started the 1981 season in the same old tired way, losing two of their first three games. But then the team caught fire and reeled off seven straight wins, including a 45–14 devastation of the Dallas Cowboys, a team that had humiliated the 49ers 59–14 just a year earlier. With two TD tosses, Joe had played a big hand in lassoing the Cowboys. After the win Walsh told reporters not to get overly excited. "We're maturing, but it will take another draft or two before we are a Super Bowl team."

The sixth game in the winning streak was special to Joe because it was against the Pittsburgh Steelers in Three Rivers Stadium, only a thirty-minute ride from where Joe had spent his boyhood. And although Joe had followed the great Steeler teams of the 1970's and had lived so close to the stadium, he had never been in it until he walked onto the field for the pregame warm-up.

In addition to the nostalgia factor, though, was Joe's realization that if the 49ers could beat the Steelers, who still had the nucleus of the team that had won Super Bowl XIV two years earlier, then the 49ers were for real.

After a three-point loss to the Cleveland Browns at San Francisco's Candlestick Park, the 49ers got right back to their winning ways with a season-ending five-game streak that raised their record to 13–3 and put the team in the play-offs for the first time in nine years.

The former sad sacks were all smiles now, and Joe's play was a major factor in the new expressions they were wearing. Most football experts will tell you that it takes three years of NFL experience before a quarterback is even ready to become a starter. Joe had not only started every game; he had compiled the highest quarterback rating in the NFL and led his team to the league's best record. Curious reporters from all

24

over the country went to Walsh, wanting to know all about the young quarterback who had led the rapid transformation. "He may have the greatest football instincts I have ever seen," Walsh told them. "He's already the best at rolling out, avoiding the rush, and still finding his primary receiver. So far he's done some things we didn't expect to happen until next year or maybe even 1983." And if Walsh had a crystal ball, he'd know that he hadn't seen anything yet.

The 49ers rode two of Joe's scoring passes and two Ronnie Lott interceptions, the last of which he ran back for a touchdown, to a 38–24 opening-round play-off win against the New York Giants.

But waiting in the wings for the 49ers was "America's Team," the Dallas Cowboys. The proud Cowboys were smarting for revenge against the upstart 49ers, who had embarrassed them with the big win during the season. A lot of people, including some of the Cowboys, still didn't think that the 49ers were ready to make a run for the Super Bowl. And although it was a close game, it looked as though Dallas would take the checkered flag when they held a 27–21 lead with only 4:15 left to play.

But as the time ticked down, Joe led the 49ers from their own 11-yard line to the Dallas six. Faced with a third down and only 58 seconds showing on the clock, Joe went back to pass. But his protection broke down, and Joe had to scramble to his right as three very large Dallas defenders came bearing down on him.

Joe pump-faked once to slow the pass rush, and then, right before he was about to go out of bounds, he saw Dwight Clark racing along the back edge of the end zone. Joe released the ball just as he was about to be smothered under a half ton of Dallas defenders, but the thunderous roar of the Candlestick crowd told him everything he needed to know. Clark had caught the ball, and the 49ers were the NFC champions for the first time in their history, and on their way to the Super Bowl to meet the Cincinnati Bengals.

John Brodie, the ex-49er quarterback who had advised Walsh to draft Joe, was thrilled. "Joe Montana, I think, will become the best quarterback who ever played the game." Another impressed bystander was Roger Staubach, who had gone from quarterbacking the Cowboys to the NFL Hall of Fame. "I'll tell you, he's something special."

During the critical drive against Dallas, Joe, according to 49er guard Randy Cross, "was as calm as he was on our Family Day picnic back in training camp." But the hype and the three-ring-circus atmosphere in the two weeks leading up to the Super Bowl did put the pressure on Joe.

As soon as he took his first snap, though, Joe was totally into the game, focused on running the offense and putting points on the board against the Bengals. And Joe started tallying the points quickly, taking the ball in himself on a one-yard keeper and then connecting on an 11-yard scoring pass to running-back Earl Cooper at the end of a 92-yard drive, the longest in Super Bowl history. Two Ray Wersching field goals upped the 49ers halftime lead to 20–0, and even though the Bengals answered back with three second-half touchdowns, San Francisco had enough fuel in their tank to power their way to a 26–21 win. And Joe, who tied Joe Namath as the youngest quarterback ever to win a Super Bowl, was selected as the game's Most Valuable Player.

It looked like Joe and the 49ers, a team of mostly young veterans, were on a one-way rocket ride to the stars, but their crash down was just around the corner.

5

Crashing

History shows that most teams go into a decline the season after they win the Super Bowl, and the 49ers followed that script absolutely.

With most teams it seems to be a combination of events, involving a lack of intensity coupled with the fact that every opponent wants to knock off the defending champs. In 1982, though, a wild card was thrown into the usual shuffle when the players went on a seven-week strike after the second week of the season.

The 49ers, who had already dropped their first two games, were ripped apart as a team by the strike because there was a lack of unity among the players. Joe was in the minority, as he was against the strike, believing that the players' union wasn't fighting for the right issues.

In the first game after the strike, the 49ers came back and clipped the Cardinals' wings while Joe set a club record with 408 yards passing. But the camaraderie that had bound the team together in their Super Bowl drive had been torn apart, and the team floundered to a 3–6 record in the strike-shortened 1982 season.

In addition to the resentment of some of his teammates and the 49ers' slide backward in the NFL standings, Joe also had to start dealing with his rather sudden fame. After the Super Bowl win and the MVP selection, the demands on his time grew. And Joe, a naturally shy and quiet person, wasn't really comfortable with all the attention. He did enjoy the praise and the extra money that he received from endorsing products and appearing in commercials, but he wasn't comfortable with the constant intrusion on his personal life. "I'm not bitter—it's part of the whole package. But it gets out of control sometimes. I'm just plain Joe. People think, 'He's a star quarterback. He should do things this way or that way.' But I do things the same way you do. I eat the same way you do. I use self-service gas stations. I wash my own car."

6

Bounce Back

Joe and his 49er teammates went into the 1983 season determined to put aside their differences and come together as a team. And while they did manage to achieve unity, they never did attain long-term consistency. After an opening-day loss to the Philadelphia Eagles, they got their gears meshed and ran off four straight wins. During that stretch, in which they averaged 36 points a game, the 49ers looked unbeatable. "We're playing more as a unit offensively than we did in our Super Bowl season," said Joe. And coach Walsh was impressed. "I'm almost in awe of those guys when they play like this."

But the 49ers went into a midseason tailspin that left them with a 7–6 record and on the edge of elimination from the play-off picture. With their backs to the wall, the 49ers regrouped and ran off three consecutive wins, including a 42–17 clobbering of the Cowboys to take the NFC Western Division title.

The 49ers continued their inconsistent play in the postseason, just squeaking by the Detroit Lions, 24–23, before dropping a 24–21 heartbreaker to the Washington Redskins in the NFC championship game.

Joe had rallied the 49ers from 21 points down in the fourth quarter against the Redskins with three TD tosses, including a 76-yarder to wide receiver Freddie Solomon. The large, noisy crowd at Washington's RFK Stadium grew quiet as they sensed the tide turning against their hometown heroes.

But a series of tough calls by the officials on Washington's next possession put the 'Skins in position to kick the winning field goal with only forty seconds left in the game. The 49ers, after coming up from so far down, were devastated, not just by the loss, but by having the game decided by questionable calls. "This was the toughest loss we had ever experienced," remembers Joe. And even a year later he would say, "I never really got that loss out of my system. I couldn't [even] watch the Super Bowl that year."

But instead of allowing that loss to go on defeating them, Joe and his teammates channeled their disappointment in a positive direction. "That particular day," said Joe, "I vowed we would make it to the next Super Bowl."

And Joe's promise turned out to be more than mere words. The 49ers even practiced with intensity in training camp, and once the season began, they were a tidal wave, sweeping their way to a record-setting 15–1 record. Included in the fifteen wins was a payback victory over Washington; a 33–0 whitewashing of the Rams, their longtime divisional rivals; and blowouts against the Browns (41–7), Saints (35–3) and Vikings (51–7). And while Joe was directing the offense to a team-record 475 points, the defense did their share, holding opponents to a league-low 227 points.

The 49ers continued rolling in the play-offs, cutting the Giants down to size 21–10 as Joe more than made up for two costly interceptions by connecting on three TD tosses.

Next in line were the Chicago Bears for the NFC championship. The 49ers had been spoiling for a rematch since a season earlier, when the Bears had beaten them while talking trash throughout the game. And in the week leading up to the play-off game, some of the Chicago players were still sounding off. They were talking about stomping the 49ers and then having a good time in San Francisco while they prepared for Super Bowl XIX, which was going to be played in Stanford Stadium, about an hour's drive from San Francisco.

But the only way that any of the Chicago players got into Stanford Stadium was by buying a ticket, because the 49ers, incensed by the bigmouthed Bears, rolled over the would-be Monsters of the Midway, 23–0.

Joe and his teammates should have been the toast of the town. But all they kept hearing about was their Super Bowl opponents, the Miami Dolphins, and the Dolphins' great young quarterback, Dan Marino, who had rewritten the NFL record book by throwing 48 touchdown passes that season. (The old record had been 36.)

Joe, who doesn't seek publicity or personal attention anyway, understood why the media was spending all their time with Marino. But the absolute lopsidedness of the coverage finally got to Joe. "You don't mind being overlooked that much, but sometimes the reporters forgot there were two teams in the game. It got to all of us. Our accomplishments were being totally ignored, and for one of the few times in my career I was angry."

Joe carried that anger into the first series of the game, causing him to distort his approach and attack the Dolphin defense with long Marino-like passes that fell incomplete.

Joe then sat on the sidelines as Marino quickly led the Dolphins into field-goal range and a 3–0 lead. By the time Joe came out for the 49ers' second series of plays, though, he was in full control of his emotions and totally focused in on the 49ers' game plan. Artfully mixing his plays, Joe took his time and led the 49ers on a 78-yard drive that he finished off with a touchdown pass to reserve running-back Carl Monroe.

Marino answered that bell by connecting on five straight passes, including a TD toss that gave the Dolphins the lead again, 10–7. But Joe kept punching, leading the 49ers to three second-quarter touchdowns and a 28–16 halftime lead. In the third quarter the 49ers delivered the knockout blows with a field goal and a 16-yard scoring pass from Joe to running back Roger Craig, which made the final score 38–16.

Joe, who set Super Bowl records for passing yardage (331) and rushing yardage by a quarterback (59), was all smiles as he held up his second MVP trophy, joining NFL Hall of

Famers Bart Starr and Terry Bradshaw as the only two-time winners.

And then Joe, who had thrown for three TD's and rushed for a fourth while directing the most proficient offense in Super Bowl history up to that point, let go of some of the feelings that he had kept hidden. "All we heard all week long was Miami's offense and how are we going to stop them. Nothing was said, but we knew we had an offense too. No one was talking about how to stop us."

But as usual Joe had raised the level of his play in a championship game, showing that in the heat of the big games, he stays Joe Cool.

7

Falling Short

Joe and his teammates had visions of riding their overpowering win in Super Bowl XIX all the way to Super Bowl XX. But their season soon turned into a series of sputtering stops and starts that never got off the launching pad.

The two high points of the year for Joe, in fact, happened off the field. The first one came in February, when he married Jennifer Wallace, a model whom he met while filming a commercial. And the second came in October, when Jennifer gave birth to a daughter, Alexandra. Having a family of his own gave Joe a newfound sense of serenity and completeness.

Joe also realized that he had struck paydirt when he arrived at training camp and started working out with a rookie wide receiver named Jerry Rice. All it took was one regular-season game for Joe to know that Jerry was the real goods.

But that game, a fumble-ridden, season opening 28–21 loss to the Vikings, set a pattern for close, frustrating losses that would plague the 49ers throughout the season. The 49ers finished at 10–6, and all of their losses, except for a 16-point thrashing by the Bears, were by seven points or less. In fact, their other five losses were by a combined total of only 20 points.

Joe, though, closed the season with a flourish, passing for more than 300 yards in each of the last three games while throwing for eight touchdowns, and leading the 49ers to the two wins that they needed to secure a wild-card spot in the play-offs.

But that was the last high point in the 49ers' up-and-down season, as the Giants brought them crashing to earth for good with a 17–3 thumping in the opening round of the play-offs.

But despite the 49ers' mediocre regular-season record and first-round elimination in the play-offs, there were a lot of reasons to look forward to the next season.

Rice and running back Roger Craig had emerged as extraordinary offensive weapons. Craig became the first player in NFL history to gain more than 1000 yards both rushing *and* receiving in the same season, while Rice had racked up nearly 1000 receiving yards in his rookie season.

And, of course, there was always Joe Montana.

But then, just one game into the 1986 season, Joe suffered a devastating back injury, and he was gone. Joe, who had been having problems with his back since 1985, twisted it severely in an opening-day stomping of the Tampa Bay Buccaneers. Joe finished the game, but one week later he was in a hospital, having surgery performed to remove a ruptured disc from his lower back and to have his spinal canal widened.

It was a career-threatening injury, and no one knew if Joe would ever play football again. In the depressing, painful days immediately following the surgery, Joe even thought about retiring. And after a visit during those early days of recovery, teammates Ronnie Lott and Dwight Clark came away from the hospital thinking that Joe's playing days were history. "Joe had to use a walker to see us to the elevator, and it exhausted him," said Lott. "As soon as the doors closed, Dwight and I looked at each other and both of us were thinking, 'It's no way, ever.' It was scary and really sad."

But within a few days, Joe snapped out of his post-operative funk, ditched any thoughts about retirement, and began a strenuous rehabilitation program. For three hours a day he lifted weights, ran, swam, and performed modified sit-ups. No one, including Arthur White, the surgeon who had performed the operation, gave any thought to Joe coming back to play that season. "If I tell my patients to go play football," said Dr. White, "then I'm crazy."

But Joe had ideas of his own. "The doctors have their

schedule, and I have mine," he said. And by early October, Joe, defying all expectations, was in a park throwing footballs to his wife and a cousin. And then, after a single practice on November 3, Joe declared that he was ready to return to the line-up. It was a remarkable recovery and, for the 49ers, who had muddled along with a 4–3–1 record in Joe's absence, it came just in the nick of time.

But there was still some question as to how effective Joe would be after missing half the season, and whether his back could stand up to the pounding of NFL pass rushers. Even Joe had his doubts. "I guess this is the biggest challenge I ever faced," he said before taking the field.

Joe, though, met the challange like a champion, throwing three touchdown passes to Jerry Rice while leading the 49ers to an emphatic, 43–17, win over the Cardinals. Joe quarterbacked the team on nine possessions and, incredibly, took them in for a score on seven of those possessions.

After one of the scoring passes to Rice, Joe was pounded into the Candlestick turf by the Cardinals pass rush. Bubba Baker, a massive defensive end who had just helped knock Joe down, bent over and said admiringly, "You're a heck of a man."

With Joe back in control of the offensive reigns, the 49ers galloped to their fourth Western Division title since Joe became the full-time starter in 1981. But in the play-offs, the 49ers made the mistake of getting in the path of the Giants, who were on a rampage toward their first Super Bowl title, and the New Yorkers put a sudden sorry stop to the 49ers' season for the second straight year. The ferocious Giants defense, led by their all-world linebacker, Lawrence Taylor, applied relentless pressure on Joe until they decked him with a sack that knocked him senseless and put him out of the game, which the Giants went on to win 49–3.

Joe's season may have ended in a crumpled heap in Giants Stadium, but his courage in coming back from the injury served as an inspiration for his teammates and for other injury victims all around the country. Joe's teammates acknowledged his extraordinary valor by selecting him as the annual winner of the Len Eshmont Award for "courageous and inspirational play."

8

Hanging Tough

In 1987 Joe was forced to begin dealing with another type of ordeal, a crisis of confidence brought about by coach Walsh. It was a conflict that would continue to plague Joe throughout the 1988 season as well.

Statistically, Joe had his best year to date while leading the 49ers to a 13–2 record, tops in the NFL. (The season was shortened by one game by a players' strike.) Joe won his first passing title, led the league in TD tosses with 31, set a record by completing 22 consecutive passes, and guided the 49ers to the NFL's top yardage total.

But the sensational season ended in anguish and disappointment when the 49ers were eliminated in the opening round of the play-offs for the third consecutive year, 36–24, by the Minnesota Vikings.

Joe was having an off day against the hard-charging Vikings defense, completing only 12 of 26 passes. And Walsh, instead of giving Joe more time to get untracked, decided to yank the NFL's best quarterback and try to get the job done with his understudy, Steve Young.

Being pulled out of the Viking game had been a humiliating experience for Joe, who had contributed so much to the rise of the 49ers. And when he arrived in training camp for the 1988 season, the painful process began all over again.

Walsh took away Joe's sense of security by putting the quarterback position up for grabs between Joe and Steve, a talented left-hander with good speed who was five years younger than Joe. For the first time in his career, Joe went into games looking over his shoulder, knowing that if he hit a rough patch, Walsh was ready with the hook.

Joe was on a season-long emotional roller coaster, and his play and the team's performance went along for the ride. One week Joe would throw for over 300 yards and four TD's, as he did against the Seattle Seahawks, a performance that earned him NFC Offensive Player-of-the-Week honors. But that was followed by a three-week stretch in which Joe failed to throw a single touchdown pass.

And the 49ers, after eleven weeks of that up-and-down season, found themselves with a 6–5 record and doing a fast fade out of the play-off picture. But then Joe came to life and led the 49ers to big wins over the Redskins, helped by an 80-yard scoring strike by Joe, and the Chargers, whom Joe burnt with a 96-yard touchdown toss. And the 49ers, with Joe in full control, stretched their streak to five games and captured their third-straight NFC West title.

But despite the 49ers' strong finishing kick, their play-off prospects weren't bright. They had been beaten badly in the first round of postseason play for three consecutive seasons. And their futility had been highlighted by the failure of their three offensive superstars—Montana, Rice, and Craig—to generate a single touchdown in those three losses.

But the 49ers and their trio of superstars shook off the ghosts of those past performances in an opening-round 34–9 rout of the Vikings, the team that had upset them a year earlier. Joe connected with Rice on three first-half touchdown passes, and Craig closed out the scoring with two fourth-quarter scores, including an 80-yard romp, the longest scoring run from scrimmage in NFL postseason history.

After the game, Joe expressed the relief and satisfaction that everyone on the team was feeling. "It's been a long road to get here. There's been a lot of pressure on us for not winning the last few years in the first round."

Still standing in the 49ers' way, though, was another old nemesis, the Chicago Bears. And on game day, the weather also loomed as an opponent, as arctic winds sent the wind-chill factor down to minus 26 degrees.

But Joe and his teammates refused to bend to the Bears or the weather. On their third possession, Joe defied the swirling winds and hooked up with Rice on a long scoring pass to give the 49ers a 7–0 lead. The two stars repeated their act in the second quarter to run their lead to 14–0, and in the third quarter Joe jolted the Bears again, connecting with tight-end John Franks for his third scoring pass of the day.

After the 49ers finished beating up on the Bears, 28–3, Dan Hampton, Chicago All-Pro defensive tackle, summed up the game in one quick sentence. "They kicked our butts." And even the usually tight-lipped Walsh was all smiles. "This is as great a game as we've had in many, many years. We've played back-to-back great football games." And then he put his arm around Joe's shoulder and said, "It's one of the greatest games Joe Montana has ever played."

Walsh's words were a bittersweet potion to Joe after his season of uncertainty. Joe had suffered through two benchings and had his confidence shaken by his coach's lack of faith. "By far, this was my toughest season," said Joe, comparing it even to 1986 when he had the surgery and missed half the schedule. "This year I felt like I was trying to be counted out, and I didn't understand it. I felt like I had a good training camp, and yet there seemed to be that constant feeling that if I had a bad game or, even, a few bad series, Steve would be in there."

And even after his two masterful play-off performances had led the 49ers to Miami to meet the Bengals in Super Bowl XXIII, Joe still didn't feel secure. "I haven't reached a comfort zone where I feel the job is mine," he said at the time.

But Walsh's concerns and Joe's self-doubts weren't shared by his teammates. As reserve wide-receiver Mike Wilson noted, "Joe has poise and control on the field. He's always been calm, cool Joe. He's the best." And then Joe took the field at Joe Robbie Stadium and showed the world just what Wilson meant.

After almost three periods of defensive domination by both teams, Cincinnati took a 13–6 lead on an electrifying 93-yard kickoff return with less than a minute left in the third quarter. The Bengals were on the prowl and ready to roar. But before they had a chance to build their momentum, Joe got the points right back with three quick strikes, including a 14-yarder to Rice that tied the score at 13–13. The Bengals, though, took the lead again, 16–13, with only 3:20 left in the season. On the sidelines, some of the Cincinnati players began a premature celebration. "I figured with the way our defense was playing, it was going to be a sweet ride home," said Bengals quarterback Boomer Esiason.

But Joe had travel plans of his own. And as soon as he stepped into the huddle, according to Bubba Paris, San Fransisco's massive left tackle, "When you looked in his eyes, you could almost see the Super Bowl ring on his finger."

Starting at his own eight-yard line, Joe kept the Bengals off balance with a series of short passes. Knowing that the defense was geared to stop the sideline patterns, Joe crossed them up by passing primarily over the middle. And then, with the ball deep in Bengal territory at the 10-yard line, Joe took the snap and dropped back. First he looked to Roger Craig and then at Jerry Rice, but both of those targets had drawn double coverage. So Joe turned towards John Taylor, who was streaking into the end zone. And with only 34 clicks left on the clock, Joe threw a perfect spiral into Taylor's outstretched hands to give the 49ers a fabulous 20–16 win.

Joe, having led the 49ers to their third Super Bowl win of the 1980's, making them the team of the decade, walked off the field with a big smile on his face and his right index finger jabbing the air in a sign of triumph.

Joe had again demonstrated his awesome ability to remain calm in a chaotic situation and to perform in pressure-filled situations as though everything was happening in slow motion. Joe, though, just shrugs off the disbelief that observers feel. "All those fourth-quarter periods are really fun. They make you concentrate more."

In the dressing room, Joe, who had set a Super Bowl record with 357 passing yards, was showered with praise by both teams. Boomer Esiason said that the final drive was the greatest of all time, while Cris Collingsworth, a Cincinnati wide receiver, was awe-struck. "Joe Montana," he said, "is not human."

And Joe's teammate, center Randy Cross, wasn't satisfied with having his quarterback included among the best of all time. "He's the greatest big-game player I've seen. Period." And Doug Williams, who had quarterbacked Washington to a smashing Super Bowl win the year before, was in total agreement. "Montana proved to me that when it comes to the big games, Joe has done more than anybody who has played football."

After the season of turmoil that Joe had been through, the praise was as welcome as a warm summer day. But Joe didn't waste any time basking in the glory. While still standing in the locker room at Joe Robbie Stadium, Joe held the Vince Lombardi Trophy, which is given to the winning Super Bowl team, over his head and set the 49ers' sights on the 1989 season. "We're coming back," he announced. "We're going to repeat."

9

The Best Ever

But one person who wouldn't be going along for the ride was Bill Walsh. A few days after becoming the second-winningest coach in Super Bowl history behind Chuck Noll's four victories with the Steelers, Walsh resigned and went on to become an NFL analyst for NBC-TV. George Seifert, the 49ers' longtime defensive coordinator, was named head coach, and he made it clear from the git-go that Joe was, undisputedly, the team's quarterback.

Given that peace of mind, Joe turned in what may be the best season of quarterbacking that anyone has ever had. From the first game to the last game, 1989 was a Joe Montana highlight film.

In the season opener Joe got the 49ers off on the right foot by connecting with Rice on a 58-yard touchdown pass late in the fourth quarter to lead the 49ers past the Indianapolis Colts, 30–24. Joe took matters into his own hands in the next game, running the ball in himself for the winning score with only 40 seconds showing on the clock.

Game three was billed as a showdown between Joe and Randall Cunningham, the Eagels' rifle-armed young quarterback. Philadelphia took it to the 49ers early as they jumped out to a 21–10 lead and forced Joe out of the game with bruised ribs after sacking him *eight* times. But Joe came back big in the fourth quarter, throwing for 428 yards and 4 TD's to rally the 49ers to an electrifying 38–28 win.

After being derailed by the Rams, Joe got the 49er express back on track with three TD tosses in a 24–20 win over the Saints. Forced by injuries to sit out most of the next three games, Joe returned just in time to give the Saints a sense of déja-vu as he threw three first-half TD tosses and ran the ball in himself for a fourth-quarter score on the way to a 31–13 49er win. The following week, the Atlanta Falcons felt as if they were part of an instant replay sequence as Joe again passed for three scores and went in himself for a fourth score as the 49ers flattened the Falcolns 45–3.

Joe continued in this incredible fashion, completing his finest season ever while compiling a 112.4 quarterback rating, the highest in NFL history, and leading the 49ers to an NFL-best 14–2 record.

Joe pulled out five of those wins with fourth-quarter rallies, showing that at 33 he was still the Comeback Kid.

Joe's extraordinary efforts were rewarded by his being named the NFL's MVP for the first time in his fabled career, and being selected as the Man of the Year by *The Sporting News*.

Joe was grateful for the personal recognition, but he had his sights squarely on the Super Bowl. To Joe, team accomplishments have always come before individual awards. As Ronnie Lott said, "He's got to be the most unselfish player in the history of the game."

The first step in the 49ers' quest to become the first repeat Super Bowl winners since the Pittsburgh Steelers had turned the trick a decade earlier were the Minnesota Vikings. And although the Vikings featured the NFL's top-rated defense, Joe ripped them apart as quickly and as easily as an eager child opening a present.

After Joe connected with Jerry Rice on a first-quarter 72-yard scoring play, the Vikings seemed to shrink into a helpless shell. As Viking defensive coordinator Floyd Peters remarked, "The defense went into shock after that. It was a total collapse." And Joe didn't give the Vikes a chance to recover, leading the 49ers on four first-half scoring drives that clinched the game before the halftime whistle blew.

Next up for the 49ers after their 41–13 walkover defeat of

the Vikings was the Los Angeles Rams, for the NFC championship. The Ram players were bold and confident, announcing that this was, "the real Super Bowl," and that they were the team to stop the 49er tidal wave.

But Joe and his teammates sliced through the Rams' defense like a powerful storm through a house of straw. Joe connected on three first-half scoring passes, the last of which, to John Taylor, broke the back of the Rams' resistance. It was a typical Joe Montana buzzer-beating drive that caused LA's veteran cornerback LeRoy Irwin to concede, "That drive sent us reeling. We were on our heels the rest of the game." And the 49ers won in a breeze, 30–3.

Joe had raised his game to such an incredible level in the two play-off wins that one NFL scout said, "It was like a professional quarterback coming back to his high school and running a drill. I've never seen a quarterback make it look as easy as Joe does."

And Joe, saving his best for last, made it look easier still in New Orleans, the city known as The Big Easy, where the 49ers blew away the Denver Broncos in Super Bowl XXIV.

Joe, throwing a record-setting five touchdown passes, played a nearly perfect game in leading the 49ers to a 55–10 win, the most lopsided in Super Bowl history. "Joe's been phenomenal all year," said George Seifert. "But it seems that he's elevated his performance for the play-offs. His concentration, his 'into-it-ness'—it's mindboggling. He hasn't had a flat spot.

"You look at him from the sidelines, and you're almost in awe. You find yourself watching like a fan would."

In the locker room after the game, Joe was presented with his third Super Bowl MVP award. But having reached the goal he had sat after last year's win. Joe was already looking to Super Bowl XXV. "Each Super Bowl win is sweeter. Let's go get another."

Just two years earlier Joe's career had seemed to be in decline. And now he was being hailed by most observers as the greatest quarterback of all time. Bill Walsh, for one said, "When the game is on the line, and you need someone to go in there and win it right now, I would rather have Joe Montana as my quarterback than anybody else who has ever played the game. No one has been able to win with all the chips down like Joe." And the current 49ers' coach, George Seifert, echoed Walsh's views and provided another insight into Joe's greatness. "Here he is, this great leader, this great athlete, and he constantly credits other people. He never demeans anybody. He is always encouraging. The team responds to that. That's the reason, I think, you see them blocking them out for him.

"He is the greatest quarterback of all time."

But Joe isn't much interested in all this talk about whether he's the best quarterback ever to play the game. "I don't want to be judged that way until after I retire."

And the way Joe and the 49ers are playing, retirement will hopefully be a long ways off. As Joe recently said, "They'll have to carry me out kicking and screaming."

Joe and Jerry go over strategies with receivers coach Sherm Lewis at halftime.

Joe shows his form.

Joe setting up against the Bears in frozen Soldiers Field.

Joe and Bill Walsh discuss last minute strategy during winning drive in Super Bowl XXIII.

Joe launches a pass against the Rams in 1989 playoff win.

Joe scans the field in Super Bowl XXIV.

Jerry heads for the end zone.

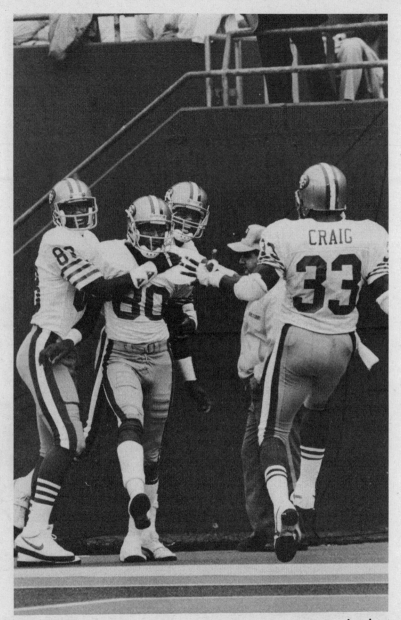

Teammates congratulate Jerry after he scores winning touchdown on the last play of the game against the Giants.

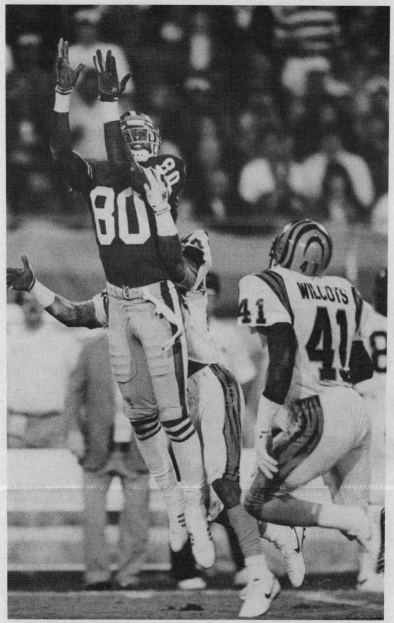
Jerry leaps for the grab against Cincinnati in Super Bowl XXIII.

Jerry leaves would-be tacklers grasping at air.

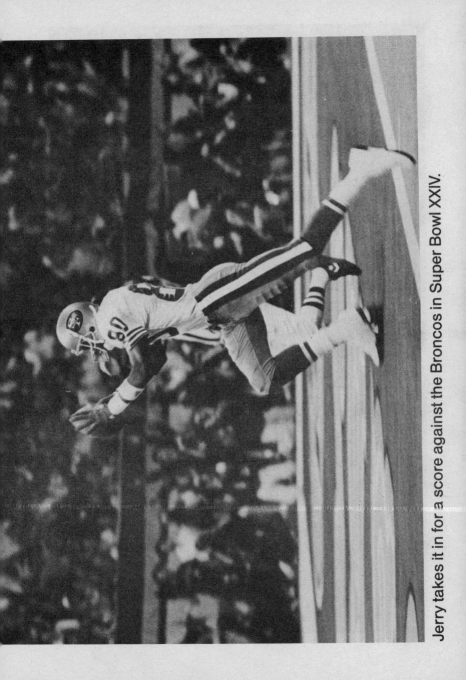

Jerry takes it in for a score against the Broncos in Super Bowl XXIV.

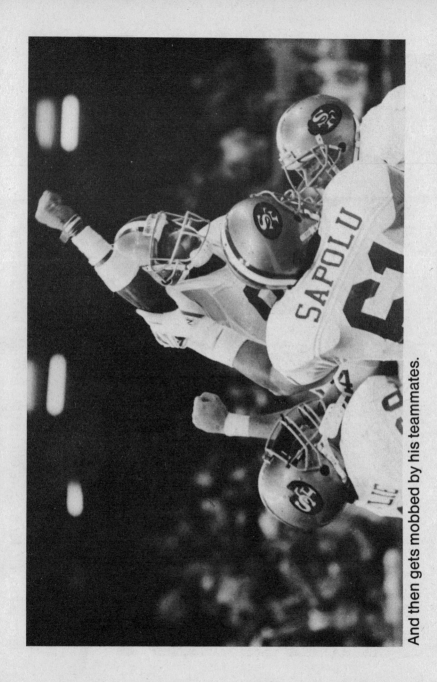

And then gets mobbed by his teammates.

JERRY RICE

1

Catching Bricks

Jerry Rice was born on October 13, 1962, in Starkville, Mississippi, and raised 35 miles away in Crawford, a tiny spot of a town of about five hundred people.

Jerry's dad, Joe, was a bricklayer who worked long, hard hours under the hot Mississippi sun, but there was never enough money for Joe and his wife, Eddie, to stretch across the eight children in the Rice family.

"If we went on a school field trip," remembers Jerry, "the other kids could buy candy and Cokes and souvenirs and things. I couldn't. It was tough to deal with."

For fun, Jerry and his five brothers would chase the neighbors' horses who grazed on the Rice's farmland. When the boys caught the horses, they would go galloping bareback across the field.

But most of the time that Jerry and his brothers were not attending school, they were out working with their father, earning needed dollars by helping him lay the bricks that went into a lot of the buildings in Oktibbeha County.

Jerry would go up on the swaying scaffolding with his dad and catch the bricks that were thrown up to him. "One of my brothers would stack about four bricks on top of each other and toss them up. They might go this way and that way, and I would catch all four." And until this day Joe maintains, "He handled bricks better than any worker I ever had. I was sorry to see him go." Even then, Jerry had the large, soft hands of a great wide receiver.

Jerry, though, was more interested in hitting the books than in hauling in footballs until he had an unexpected meeting with the vice principal of B.L. Moor High School at the beginning of his sophomore year.

One day Jerry decided to cut classes and was spotted by the vice principal. "He slipped up behind me and scared me," says Jerry. "I just took off running, and all he could see was the flash of the red jacket."

The vice principal must have been a pretty fair talent scout, though, because after dishing out the usual punishment, he suggested that Jerry could put that speed to better use on the football field, and directed "Flash" to report to the football coach. And ever since then, defensive backs at all levels, from high school to the NFL, have been paying the price for Jerry's day of truancy.

Jerry's mom, Eddie, wasn't too thrilled with the idea of one of her son's playing such a rough sport. "But the more I fought it, the more determined he was, so I gave it up." Papa Joe, though, loved watching his boys play ball, and he still remembers the day that he realized that Jerry had a special talent.

"It was just fun to watch them, Tom, Jimmy, and Jerry. They were always after that football. One day I saw Jerry dive into a thorn bush after a ball. He got stuck bad, but he caught it. When I saw that, I felt something."

2

World

Jerry went on to become a high-school gridiron star, snaring 35 touchdown passes in his senior year. But no college coaches came to beat down the Rices' door. Jerry was especially disappointed by the lack of interest shown by Mississippi State, which was located just a few miles down the road from the Rice home. "I grew up wanting to go to Mississippi State more than anything in the world. But they didn't even care enough to write." Jerry's short-term pain turned out to be State's long-term embarrassment, though, for allowing such a great talent to go unnoticed in their own backyard.

One school that did show a little interest was Mississippi Valley State, a small, predominantly black college about 100 miles away from Crawford in a town called Itta Bena. But the interest was so slight that Archie Cooley, the head coach at the time, didn't go to see Jerry play until the football season had finished and he was already pounding the boards for Moor's basketball team.

But once Cooley saw Jerry's athleticism, he couldn't wait to see him in an MVS uniform. "I became impressed with him immediately. He could jump through the roof, and he had those huge hands. He got about thirty points that night, and right away I decided we had to have him."

Jerry's talents were perfectly suited to the offensive schemes of "Gunslinger" Cooley, whose motto was "The fastest way between two points is to fly."

And Jerry flew, catching 30 passes in his freshman year, and more than doubling that total in his sophomore year. "I just felt natural right away," said Jerry, who was nicknamed by his teammates "World," as in "All-World." "Then things just started getting easier." But the only reason that things got easier was because of how hard Jerry worked.

Jerry kept improving, because he wasn't content to rely on his natural speed and exceptional jumping ability. He participated in a sprinting program to improve his quickness and a weight-training program to increase his strength. Jerry also worked at developing his concentration and learning to run precise pass patterns. And you could usually find him running his routes an hour before practice even officially began. All this extra effort by Jerry wasn't at all surprising, for as his mother said, "He has worked hard at everything he's done all his life."

Jerry quickly became the marked man in the Delta Devil's offense, usually having to defeat double- or even triple-teaming, but he made it sound as though it was as easy to deal with as a quiet stroll through the park. "You've got to get rid of the first man, run the pattern on the second man, and take the ball away from the third man." Just like that.

And after Jerry had the ball, he was bad news for any defensive back who was between him and the goal line. "He comes across the field with so much intensity that guys seem like they are getting out of *his* way," remarked Gloster Richardson, the Delta Devils' receiving coach, and an ex-pro star with the Kansas City Chiefs. And Jerry relished those open-field opportunities. "I'm always looking to turn it upfield and run over some people."

Jerry ran over lots of people while catching over one hundred passes in each of his last two seasons, including an astounding 28 touchdown receptions in his senior year. By the time Jerry hung up his Delta Devils' cleats, he had set 18 NCAA Division 1-AA records, including career yardage and touchdown totals, and the pro scouts were paying a lot more attention than the college coaches had four years earlier.

Dick Steinberg, a longtime NFL talent evaluator and currently the general manager of the New York Jets, seemed to feel that there wasn't any limit to Jerry's potential. "You'd see him catch ten in the first half, and you wondered if he could catch thirty in a game," said Steinberg with a straight face.

One of the teams that had a particular interest in Jerry was the 49ers. They were looking for a long-range wide receiver who could stretch defensive secondaries and take the pressure off the short-range passing schemes that Bill Walsh favored.

The 49ers sent Paul Hackett, an offensive assistant at the time, to watch Jerry work out with hundreds of other college senior who had dreams of playing in the NFL. "Jerry was sensational. I couldn't believe what I was watching. I couldn't wait to get back to Bill [Walsh] and tell him what I'd seen."

The only problem was that the 49ers, coming off their win in Super Bowl XIX, would have the 28th pick in the draft, too late to grab Jerry. So, on the day of the draft, Walsh traded the team's top three draft picks to the New England Patriots to move up in the draft and get their man.

Jerry, who had been watching the draft on TV with one of his brothers, was thrilled. "My first thought was, 'Super Bowl champs. I'm going to get one of those rings for myself.' "

3

Rookie

Jerry had the normal case of rookie shakes in his first season, trying to earn a spot on a veteran team. Jerry, though, also had to deal with being a long way from home for the first time, and adjusting to big-city ways after spending his entire life in small-town rural settings. "When I got here, things didn't really fall in place for me. I remember stepping off the plane. At that particular moment, I wanted to turn around and go back on the plane because of the shyness. I had a hard time. I kept my head in the right frame of mind, though. If not for that, I'd probably be home in Mississippi."

Jerry handled the pressure with remarkable maturity and demonstrated, almost immediately, that his talents as a receiver were something special.

Paul Hackett remembers a catch that was so spectacular that, even though it was an exhibition game and Jerry came down out of bounds, he says, "I'll never forget it. He went up between three defenders, got bumped, and still came down with the ball. It seemed like he could just hang there in the air forever on that pass, waiting for the ball. It's one of the greatest catches I've ever seen."

Jerry also caught Joe Montana's attention in the first regular-season game when he went across the middle and made a great leaping catch. "Jerry showed everyone that he wasn't afraid to go across the middle—the most dangerous spot for a receiver—to catch a pass," Montana said.

The 49ers, though, brought Jerry along slowly, easing him into the lineup gradually so as to lessen the pressure on him. But despite the coaching staff's best-laid plans, Jerry still hit a midseason patch in which he dropped a lot of catchable balls, causing his confidence to sag. "I started dropping passes in my sleep. It was tough to deal with. I couldn't concentrate on the football. I was thinking about the offense, my pattern, and what the defense was trying to do to me."

Jerry, though, dealt with the situation head-on, working harder in practice and learning the offense more completely, so that he didn't have to continually think about what he was supposed to do and could just concentrate on beating his defender and catching the ball.

Jerry's efforts paid off so well that by the fourteenth game of the season, he grabbed ten passes, including a 66-yard touchdown catch, for a whopping 241 yards, a new 49er record. Steve Shafer, the Rams' defensive-backfield coach who had just seen his secondary get eaten alive, had had enough of the 49ers' talented rookie. "The thing he does is finish a play as well as anyone in football. He goes for the ball better than anybody, and he knows what to do with it when he catches it."

Jerry closed out the season with another big game against Dallas and walked away with the United Press International Rookie of the Year Award, as well as the National Football League Players' Association Offensive Rookie of the Year. But his dream of winning a Super Bowl ring was short-circuited by the Giants in the opening round of the play-offs.

Jerry had shown the league that a new star was emerging, but without a crystal ball, no one would have guessed that he was about to ignite with all the brightness of a supernova.

4

Sophomore Sensation

For some unknown reason a lot of professional athletes who have fine rookie seasons seem to slump their second season. Aware of this phenomenon, Jerry spent the offseason working out and building himself up so that he wouldn't fall victim to the "sophomore jinx" for lack of effort.

Jerry did take some time off, though, to arrange to have a new home built for his parents. "They didn't have much when I was growing up, but all they had went to the kids. When I got to the NFL, I was determined to give something back to them. This is it," said Jerry.

Despite Jerry's offseason dedication and an excellent training-camp effort, it looked like the jinx was going to get Jerry on an end-around play when Joe Montana went down with the back injury that would sideline him for half of the 49ers' 1986 schedule.

It takes a lot of experience for a receiver and a quarterback to learn each other's moves and develop the timing and knowledge that allows them to work smoothly together. So the loss of a starting quarterback is usually a setback to any receiver, but especially a young and relatively inexperienced wide receiver still trying to master the intricacies of a Bill Walsh defense.

But Jerry adapted to the change without missing a beat. In the 49ers' first game after the injury, Jerry hauled in six passes for 155 yards, including a 66-yard touchdown against the Rams. Jerry followed up that performance with a two-touchdown effort against the Dolphins, and two spectacular back-to-back beauties against the Colts and Vikings in which he collected 13 passes good for 316 yards and five more touchdowns.

The speed with which Jerry turned into such a dangerous receiver startled even the 49ers. "There is no better player at his position right now than Jerry Rice," declared Bill Walsh. "There are some as good, but none better. We always said that his best would come three or four years down the road, but he's surprised us all."

Joe Montana also caught everyone by surprise when he returned to the lineup in time for the 49ers' tenth game of the season. Jerry did his part to welcome Joe back by hauling in three touchdown passes and racking up 157 yards in receptions. It did more for Joe's spirits than a Hallmark card.

The following week the 49ers played in Washington, and Jerry had his biggest game of the season against the 'Skins and their All-Pro cornerback, Darrell Green. Jerry made the speedy Green look like a confused rookie as he burned him 12 times for 204 yards, one of only two 200-plus-yard performances turned in by an NFL receiver in 1986. After the game a shame-faced Green admitted, "I'm embarrassed."

Jerry went on to embarrass a lot of other cornerbacks throughout the league, finishing the season with 86 receptions good for a league-leading 15 touchdown grabs and 1,570 receiving yards, the third highest total ever in the long history of the NFL.

Jerry's accomplishments earned him All-Pro honors and a selection as *Sports Illustrated*'s NFL Player of the Year, a rare honor for a second-year performer.

"Jerry's become so good so fast, it scares you sometimes," said Dennis Green, the 49ers' receivers coach at the time. "He just explodes towards the ball. If a pass is near him, it's his. He just turns on the afterburners.

"And he has a basketball player's leaping ability. If he goes up in a crowd with two or three defenders, Jerry's going to get the ball. And if both of them grab it at once, Jerry will probably pull it away. He's a tough kid."

Tough enough, too, to have beaten the sophomore jinx in a big, big way.

But it was a different story in the 49ers' play-off game against the Giants. Lawrence Taylor and his playmates, who would go on to win the Super Bowl that year, just rolled over the 49ers and flattened them out, 49–3.

The game was a horror show for the 49ers from start to finish. For Jerry, though, there was one play that stood out like a bad dream. In the first quarter, the 49ers had the chance to strike first and take the early lead. They were in Giant territory and driving towards a touchdown as Jerry pulled down a slant-in pass and headed for the end zone. "I was actually pulling away from the defense and thinking about the touchdown giving us the lead, thinking about bang-spiking it in the end zone."

But as Jerry crossed the 20-yard line, the ball fell out of his hand and rolled into the end zone, where a Giant player fell on it. "It just came out," said Jerry, speaking about the only ball he had fumbled all year.

Most of the people who watched the game thought it was a bizarre but insignificant play, thinking that even if Jerry hadn't fumbled, the Giants were so domineering that the final score still wouldn't have been closer than 49–10 anyway.

But some people, including Jerry, wonder whether that early score could have changed the momentum and the outcome of the game. "You tell yourself that you lost so badly that it doesn't matter, but you never know. That one play might have given us all we needed to win the game. That one play might have put us in the Super Bowl. It will always linger in the back of my mind." When he made his travel plans for the Pro-Bowl game, he made sure that he'd be airborne while the Super Bowl was being televised. "I didn't want to know anything about that game."

Although Jerry's sophomore year may have ended on a down note, one dropped ball couldn't obscure his season-long display of brilliance or slow his relentless pursuit of greatness.

5

Touchdown Machine

Instead of sitting around and brooding about the dropped ball, Jerry went to work getting ready for the 1987 season. He reported to training camp in great shape, ready to put in the time and effort that would allow him to take his game to the next level.

"Jerry's like everyone else," said Dennis Green, a 49er assistant at the time. "But he works *hard*. He stays after practice day after day. The guy's always improving, and he's almost perfect now."

Ronnie Lott, who has always set the highest standards, also spoke admiringly of the way that Jerry goes all out, even in practice. "Jerry's always at top speed. Young defensive backs want to avoid him in drills."

And then, comparing Jerry to two Hall of Fame receivers, Lott added, "Covering Jerry in practice is the closest I'll ever come to covering a Paul Warfield or Charlie Taylor."

And the NFL Hall of Fame is where Jerry has set his sights. Jerry had a chance to visit the Hall when the 49ers opened their exhibition schedule with a game in Canton, Ohio, and he came away inspired. "It sent chills through me. That's where I want to go. I want to be in there with guys who didn't play for the money as much as for the challenge."

Once the regular season started, Jerry showed that in only his third year he was already the equal of any of the immortals elected to the Hall of Fame.

Playing in only 12 games because of a players' strike, Jerry lived up to his nickname of "World" by setting a record for touchdown receptions, with 22. Jerry *shattered* the old standard of 18 touchdown receptions that Miami's Mark Clayton had established over a 16-game schedule in 1984, the year that Dan Marino was filling the air with footballs.

Jerry's total of 23 touchdowns (he also ran one in on a reverse play against the Atlanta Falcons) left him one shy of the league record of 24, set by former Washington running back John Riggins, but the 138 points that he tallied gave him the NFL scoring title, the first time a wide receiver had led the league since Hall of Famer Elroy "Crazy Legs" Hirsch had done it in 1951.

Jerry's accomplishment was so awesome that people were searching for new adjectives to describe his all-world performance. Tim McKyer, his teammate at the time, captured the image as well as anyone. "You feed all the data of the ideal receiver into a computer and it spits out Jerry Rice."

Jerry also set another record by catching at least one touchdown in 13 consecutive games, including the last game of the 1986 season and all 12 games that he played in 1987. "For a receiver to have that kind of consistency is remarkable," said Lynn Swann, a former All-Pro on the Steelers' Super Bowl teams of the seventies. To Bill Walsh, in fact, the consecutive-game streak was an even more outstanding achievement than the 23 touchdowns that Jerry had scored over 12 games.

Jerry's fabulous season began in Pittsburgh, where the 49ers opened with a loss to the Steelers. After the game, Steeler cornerback Dwayne Woodruff seemed relieved that Jerry had caught only one touchdown pass against him. "Covering Rice is like a horror show. He's so smooth when he's running. He gets right on you, and before you know it, he's by you. Once he is, I don't think anybody's going to catch him."

The following week Jerry saved the 49ers from going into a tailspin when he caught his second touchdown pass of the game with no time showing on the clock to boost the 49ers over the Bengals, 27–26.

Following four weeks of forced vacation because of the players' strike, Jerry kept his streak alive with one touchdown grab in each of the 49ers' next three games. And then Jerry closed with a fabulous finishing kick by scoring *16 touchdowns* in his last *seven games,* all of which the 49ers won. During that sensational stretch, Jerry scored three touchdowns in three of the games and two more in three other games. Only one team, the Green Bay Packers, held him to a single touchdown in that span.

After Jerry burned the Tampa Bay Buccaneers for three touchdowns, their head coach, former NFL wide receiver Ray Perkins, didn't need to see any more. "He's the best receiver in football."

The following week's foe, the Cleveland Browns, hadn't become believers—yet. Before the game, Hanford Dixon, one of their two All-Pro cornerbacks, laid down the challenge. "We're going to stay in his face all day." That tough talk just made Jerry's teammate, Randy Cross, smile. "He's more confident when people say what they're going to try to do to him. It seems to goad him into playing better."

Then Jerry went out and proved Cross correct by burning the Browns for seven catches, including three more touchdown receptions, as the 49ers creamed Cleveland, 38–24. The only effective defense against Jerry was the game officials, who forced him to get rid of his good-luck towel, which had "Flash 80" written on it. "They took away my energy," said Jerry after the game. But then he found a way to restore his elixir by taping the message on the bottom of his cleats. And at least that way, Dixon and the rest of the league's cornerbacks had something to read while Jerry raced into the end zone.

Jerry's extraordinary efforts helped the 49ers achieve an NFL-best 13–2 record (including three wins by a team of strikebreakers that counted in the official standings). But for the third consecutive year, the 49ers were routed in their opening-round play-off game. This time the villain was the Vikings, and once again the 49ers' celebrated trio of scoring stars—

Montana, Craig, and the Touchdown Machine, Jerry Rice—failed to produce a single score.

Joe took most of the heat from the fans and the media, especially after Walsh replaced him mid-game with Steve Young.

But Jerry, who played the game hampered by a pulled muscle and a bad knee, leaped to Montana's defense. "Everyone said Joe had a bad game. Well, *everybody* did. I had three or four balls that I didn't come down with that I should have had. It's disappointing to me that I didn't play better."

And even though Jerry was named the NFL's Most Valuable Player and the *Sporting News* NFL Player of the Year, the early elimination from the play-offs cut deeply. As Jerry said, "The only thing I have to hang on to is the awards. The season didn't end like I wanted it to."

It was beginning to look as though the only way Jerry was going to get to a Super Bowl was to buy a ticket.

6

Over the Hump

Jerry had roared like a lion during his first three seasons in the NFL, but had been as quiet as a mouse in the play-offs. Jerry was disturbed at his, and the team's, poor performance in those three-straight postseason losses.

When it had counted most, Jerry and the 49ers' other two offensive superstars, Joe Montana and Roger Craig, had produced the least. The trio had rewritten the record book during the previous three seasons, but had failed to produce a single touchdown in postseason play. In those three opening-round losses, Jerry had been limited to a total of only ten catches for 121 yards. It was beginning to look as though he might never get to wear the Super Bowl ring that he had thought about back on draft day in 1985.

And after the 49ers floundered their way through the first 11 games of the 1988 season, it didn't look as though they would even make it to the play-offs. With a 6–5 record and only five games to go, their hopes were down to a faint flicker.

The usually explosive offense of the 49ers sputtered as Joe Montana struggled through his most miserable and least productive season, while Jerry suffered an injury to his right ankle in the team's seventh game that hampered him for the remainder of the season.

Jerry, though, came up big in the 49ers' four-game stretch drive that turned their season around. Playing through the team's turmoil and the pain of his injured ankle, Jerry came up with four touchdown grabs, including a team-record 96-yarder, as the 49ers fought their way into the play-offs. Jerry's final statistics weren't as glittering as they had been in the two previous record-setting seasons, but they were good enough to earn him All-Pro honors for the third consecutive year.

The 49ers' first play-off obstacle was the Minnesota Vikings, the team that had eliminated them a year earlier and had the NFL's top-rated defense. The 49ers, however, also had to overcome the cloud of doubt caused by their recent play-off failures.

Jerry quickly made sure that the sun shined brightly over San Francisco's Candlestick Park, though, by personally dismantling the league's dominant defense. Completely dispelling the idea that he wasn't a big-game performer, Jerry went out and tied a postseason record by scoring three times—all in the first half—leading the 49ers past the Vikes 34–9.

The 49ers had put their play-off blues behind them, but waiting in Chicago to ambush their NFC championship hopes were the big bad Bears—and NFL history. Going back to 1950, there had been 19 games in which a warm-weather team or a team that played in a domed stadium had traveled to a cold-weather city to play for a championship. And 18 times in those 19 games, the team that played in the cold-weather city had walked off its field as a winner.

But Jerry wasn't interested in the past, or in the fact that the Bears had beaten the Niners 10–9 earlier in the season. "The first time we played the Bears this year, I had a bad ankle. I couldn't really move. But I'm healthy now and I'm going to have a big game tomorrow. You're going to see a different Jerry Rice tomorrow," he announced.

Jerry also didn't allow a frigid weather forecast for the Windy City to bother him. "I don't care. I'll catch the ball in any kind of weather."

But Jerry wasn't expecting the arctic conditions that sent the temperature plunging below zero while swirling winds were whipping footballs around like wiffle balls.

The elements seemed to dictate a low-scoring, defensive

struggle without much passing. But midway through the first quarter, Jerry started delivering on his pregame promise.

On a third down and ten from their own 39-yard line, Joe sent Jerry out on a 20-yard sideline pattern. Just before the pass reached Jerry, the ball seemed to soar on a sudden updraft like a Frisbee caught in the wind. But "World," looking like he had been launched, went right up after the ball and snatched it out of the air and away from Chicago cornerback Mike Richardson. It was already a great play, but Jerry wasn't finished. As soon as his feet touched the ground, he put a fantastic fake on Todd Krumm, who had come over to make the tackle, and—*whoosh*—Jerry was gone, 61 yards, for the game's opening score.

In the second quarter, Jerry kept a drive alive by taking a short pass and turning it into a 20-yard gain. Five plays later, from the Bears' 27-yard line, Jerry, running a short slant-in pattern, snatched a knee-high bullet pass with his fingertips and sprinted the final 15 yards to the end zone. The touchdown gave the 49ers a 14–0 lead on their way to putting the Bears in the deep freeze in a big way, 28–3.

Jerry had beaten the play-off jinx for the second time, withstood the worst weather conditions he had ever played in, and completely devastated Chicago's defense. Now the only thing standing between Jerry and his Super Bowl ring was the Cincinnati Bengals.

7

Going For the Ring

The weather in Miami, the site of Super Bowl XXIII, was a big improvement over what the 49ers had faced in Chicago. But the barrage of bad-mouthing that the Bengals' defensive backs heaped on Jerry was as welcoming as an Alaskan blizzard.

The Bengals' secondary, which billed itself as "The Swat Team," kept bragging to the media that they would blanket Jerry. "We'll play a lot of bump-and-run," said Cincinnati cornerback Lewis Billups. "He won't be able to handle that." And strong safety David Fulcher added, "All of us are faster than he is."

"This isn't a track meet. It's a football game," answered Jerry, who had been hearing about his lack of speed for a long time.

His supposed lack of speed was one of the reasons that he hadn't been highly recruited by colleges, and why two other wide receivers, Al Toon (by the Jets) and Eddie Brown (by the Bengals), had been picked ahead of him in the 1985 draft.

Jerry has never liked to run in shorts against a clock, so he doesn't do the 4.2-second times that coaches like to see for a wide receiver. But in full football gear, running a pass pattern with the ball out in front of him, Jerry becomes a burner. As Ronnie Lott noted, "Jerry's got game speed. It's hard to explain, but *nobody* outruns Jerry in a game."

Most people expected Super Bowl XXIII to be a high-scoring game that would be dominated by two explosive offenses. But the fireworks fizzled early, and the teams went to their locker rooms tied at 3–3.

Jerry, with a series of acrobatic catches—including a one-handed sideline grab of a tipped ball—that were all highlight-film material, had put on a truly awesome display of pass catching in the first half. But a disputed dropped pass by Mike Wilson at the Bengals' two-yard line, a botched field goal attempt, and a fumble by Roger Craig had undercut Jerry's effort to put more points on the scoreboard.

The miscues looked as though they might prove fatal, when the Bengals broke a 6–6 tie on a 93-yard kickoff return by Stanford Jennings with less than a minute left in the third quarter.

But before Cincinnati could take control of the game, Jerry, with major contributions from Joe Montana and Roger Craig, broke the Bengals' momentum.

On the first play from scrimmage after Jennings's touchdown jaunt, Jerry took a short sideline pass from Joe, spun away from a tackle, and turned it into a 31-yard gain.

On the next play, the first of the fourth quarter, Joe connected with Craig on a 40-yard gain to take the ball to the Bengals' 14-yard line. One play later, Jerry gathered in a sideline pass in the left flat at the Bengals' five-yard line. As soon as Jerry caught the ball, Billups banged him in the back and sent him sprawling across the end line. But just before Jerry fell out of bounds, he somehow lunged forward while reaching back with his right hand and arching the football around the pylon in the corner of the end zone, to pull the 49ers into a 13–13 tie. As the 49ers' receivers coach Dennis Green said admiringly, "Everything was out of bounds except the ball."

Jerry made another unbelievable catch on the 49ers' next possession as he exploded into the air over "He won't be able to handle that" Billups, and brought down a 44-yard rainmaker. The 49ers, though, wasted that opportunity when Mike Cofer missed a 49-yard field-goal attempt.

But the extraordinary play that Jerry had made in scoring the tying touchdown on the previous series had given the 49ers the platform from which to spring back after Cincinnati retook the lead, 16–13, with only 3:20 left to play.

The 49ers went on an electrifying 92-yard scoring drive to win the most exciting Super Bowl ever played. In that drive, Jerry caught three passes that contributed 51 yards, including a key 27-yarder on a second-down-and-20 play that moved the ball to the Bengals 18-yard stripe with less than a minute left to play in the game. "I love to be in a situation like that, where everything is on the line. I want to be the guy to come up with the catch," said Jerry.

Two plays later, with the Bengals' defense keying on Jerry, John Taylor was able to get free in the end zone, where he cradled the pass that won Super Bowl XXIII for the 49ers.

Taylor acknowledged the fact that his teammate had opened up the passing lane for him. "Everyone in the place was probably looking at Jerry, not at me." Which was not surprising, since Jerry had tied one Super Bowl record with his 11 catches, including three that were in the category of unbelievable, and set a new mark with 215 receiving yards. Including the Vikings and Bears games, Jerry had caught 21 passes for 409 yards and a record tying six postseason touchdowns. No one would ever say that Jerry couldn't play in the big games again.

After Jerry left the field, he went to his locker and wept forcefully for a few minutes, mentally retracing the long, hard road that he had traveled to achieve this moment.

He remembered catching bricks out of the air, and his hard-working parents, who had loved and supported him throughout his life.

Then Jerry wiped his eyes and joined his celebrating teammates just in time to learn that he had been selected as the Most Valuable Player in the Super Bowl. Jerry modestly suggested that Joe might have been a better choice, but no one was more deserving that Jerry. As Ronnie Lott put it, "I've said all along that Jerry Rice is the best wide receiver ever to play the game. Yes, ever." And he saved one of his best performances for the most important game that he had ever played.

Jerry joined Lynn Swann (for the Steelers in Super Bowl X) and Fred Biletnikoff (for the Raiders in Super Bowl XI) as the only wide receivers to ever win the MVP award. "Lynn Swann was my idol," said Jerry. "It amazed me how he would fly through the air and make catches."

But these days it's Swann who is doing the admiring. "There isn't a wide receiver who has played a better Super Bowl to date, and that includes me," said Swann after watching Jerry soar to new heights.

Over in the Bengals' locker room, the Swat Team was still talking, but this time with respect instead of derision. "I should have played better, I guess," said Billups. "But Rice made a couple of super catches when I was right on him. I was right on him and he *still* made the catches."

David Fulcher swiftly summed up his reaction to Jerry's record-smashing performance. "Jerry Rice is in another world at times."

When Jerry was asked to comment on all the trash the Bengals' defensive backs had thrown his way, he just smiled and said, "I don't talk a game; I just go out and play."

And according to Dwight Clark, for one, Jerry plays wide receiver better than anyone who ever played the position. "The first time I saw him, he was the best I ever saw, and I learned how to turn on the television at an early age. Jerry's like a Michael Jordan, a Joe Montana. He's a step above the field."

8

Getting Better All the Time

After only four seasons in the league, Jerry was being favorably compared with the greatest receivers of all time. He had strung together four of the best seasons that any wide receiver ever had, which included: Rookie of the Year honors in his first season; achieving the third-highest receiving yardage total in NFL history in his second year; establishing the record for touchdown receptions in a season and being named the NFL's MVP during his third year; and being named the Most Valuable Player in Super Bowl XXIII in his fourth season.

Jerry, though, didn't have any interest in resting on his accomplishments and admiring his trophy case. In fact, the only ball that Jerry has kept is the one that he caught for his first NFL touchdown. "I don't want to stop and think about my other individual achievements, or it might distract me."

What Jerry stays focused on is helping the 49ers win as many championships as possible, and one day, a long time down the road, being elected to the NFL Hall of Fame.

Superstars like Jerry and Joe Montana, or Michael Jordan and Magic Johnson, aren't interested in what they've already done; they stoke their competitive fires by stepping forward to meet the next set of challenges. And they're constantly working to develop their natural talents to their fullest potential.

So instead of allowing his head to swell with praise during the offseason, Jerry cut back on the junk food that he loves and lost 15 pounds, becaused he decided that he could improve his quickness if he was lighter. And to make sure that he didn't lose strength as a result of the lost weight, Jerry put in a lot of time in the weight room, bulking up his body. "You see a lot of guys that catch the ball just fall down to the ground. But that's something we [Jerry and his teammate and fellow wide receiver, John Taylor] try to stay away from.

"If we catch the football, we're going to do something with it."

And Jerry started doing things on the opening day of the 1989 season when he caught a pass and galloped 58 yards to give the 49ers a come-from-behind win over the Colts, 30–24.

That win set the tone for the Niners' best-in-the-NFL 14–2 season. Jerry also went on to have another monster year, compiling league highs in receiving yardage (1,483) and touchdown receptions (17), including scores that put the winning points on the board in five of the Niners' 14 wins.

Jerry also set the tone for the team's drive to Super Bowl XXIV in its opening play-off contest against Minnesota.

After the Vikes jumped out to a 3–0 first-quarter lead, Jerry turned the game around with a 72-yard score that sucked the air out of the Vikings' top-rated defense.

The play started off as a simple five-yard hook pass, and finished in the end zone, as Jerry turned on the retro rockets after blasting his way out of the grasp of two would-be tacklers. The Vikes, thinking that they were watching an instant replay of what Jerry had done to them in the 1988 play-offs, reacted as if they were in shock.

Jerry made sure that they stayed in their shell by catching a 13-yard touchdown pass that increased the 49ers' halftime lead to 27–3 and put the game out of the Vikings' reach.

Jerry didn't play the starring role in the Niners' NFC championship win over the Rams, but he was the games' leading receiver and he kept the Rams' secondary so preoccupied with his whereabouts that it opened up the field for the other 49ers. And Jerry, who is probably the league's best blocking wide receiver, also helped by throwing a couple of bone-crushing blocks that twice sprang Roger Craig for big-yardage gains.

The scene of Super Bowl XXIV switched from Miami to New Orleans, but the Denver Broncos' secondary sang the same old song that the Bengals' defensive backs had sung prior to Super Bowl XXIII. This time around, free-safety Steve Atwater, the NFL's defensive Rookie of the Year, and Dennis Smith, Denver's Pro-Bowl-caliber strong safety, two of the league's hardest hitters, provided the lyrics.

"We're going to beat Rice and Taylor up a bit," Smith told reporters. "They really haven't been hit a lot in the play-offs. But when they catch a ball against us, they are going to remember it."

Jerry, hearing what was said, shot right back. "I'm ticked off. It's the same as Cincinnati last year. They talked and talked, and this game is not about talking."

With less than five minutes gone in the game, Jerry showed everyone just what the game was about. With the ball at the Denver 20, Jerry ran a slant-in pattern and caught a pass in full stride at the seven yard line, where Atwater tried to take his head off with a flying tackle. But Jerry bounced out of Atwater's grasp, juked past another defender, and ran in for the score. "I just tried to keep my balance and focus on getting into the end zone," said Jerry. "This team expects me to make a big play to get things started. I focused on that and nothing else.

"We made our minds up that we weren't going down on the first hit today. It felt awfully good."

And in case Jerry plays in any future Super Bowls, 49ers' center Jesse Sapolu has some advice. "I think everyone should learn one thing. Don't say anything about Rice before you have to play against him in a Super Bowl."

Two possessions later, the 49ers went 54 yards in ten plays to up their lead to 13–3. Jerry didn't score the touchdown, but he did set it up with two big receptions, a 20-yarder, and then a 21-yarder to dig the Niners out of a third-down hole.

Roger Craig and fullback Tom Rathman did all the work on the 49ers' third scoring drive, with Rathman ramming the ball in from the one-yard line.

Jerry got back into the scoring column just before the half ended, on a 38-yard touchdown play that had the Broncos shaking their heads. Faking a slant-in, which drew the over-anxious Denver secondary up, Jerry ran a deep post pattern behind an outclassed Dennis Smith and caught a perfect spiral to give the 49ers a 27–3 halftime lead.

Over on the sidelines, Wade Phillips, Denver's frustrated defensive coordinator, was thinking, "We worked on that play every day in practice. We knew it was coming and we still couldn't stop it."

Two minutes into the third quarter, Jerry struck again, catching a 28-yard touchdown toss that upped the 49ers' lead to 34–3 and shut the door on any hopes that Denver had of coming back.

"We just couldn't handle him," confessed Wade Phillips after the 49ers had finished demolishing Denver, 55–10. But no one has learned how to handle Jerry, who seems like a cobra, able to mesmerize his prey before striking with deadly quickness.

Jerry, as usual, was modest about his accomplishments, which included the single-game Super Bowl record of three touchdown receptions as well as the career record of four. "To win it back to back," he said about the 49ers' wins in Super Bowls XXIII and XXIV, but also to win it for this football team—that's what important."

Other people, though, including the 49ers' offensive coordinator, Mike Holmgren, wanted to talk about Jerry's greatness. "Jerry is still young, and as hard as it is to believe, I think his best years are ahead of him. He can get better, and that's a little scary."

And even in the midst of the team's locker-room celebration, Jerry was already planning ahead. "There's always room for improvement. The goal is always to get better.

"It's great winning back-to-back Super Bowls, but maybe next year we'll get another opportunity. I'm looking down the road. If you want to keep getting better, you have to set high standards for yourself."

And the standards that Jerry has set for himself are the all-time records that Steve Largent set in his 14 seasons with the Seattle Seahawks. Largent left the game following the 1989 season as the NFL's career leader in receptions (816), receiving yardage (13,035) and touchdown receptions (100). "I'm shooting for one guy, and that's Steve Largent. I feel that if I keep working hard and just keep down to earth, I might have a chance of surpassing him one day."

Those are the targets that Jerry has set his sights on, and five years into his career he's on target to achieve his goals and become the greatest receiver ever to play the game of football.

JOE MONTANA

PRO STATISTICS

		Passing								Rushing				
	G/S	ATT	COMP	YDS	PCT	LONG	INT	TD	NFL RATG	ATT	YDS	AVG	LONG	TD
1979	16/1	23	13	96	.565	18	0	1	80.9	3	22	7.3	13	0
1980	15/7	273	176	1795	.645	71t	9	15	87.8	32	77	2.4	11	2
1981	16/16	488	311	3565	.637	58t	12	19	88.2	25	95	3.8	20t	2
1982	9/9	346	213	2613	.616	55	11	17	87.9	30	118	3.9	21	1
1983	16/16	515	332	3910	.645	77	12	26	94.6	61	284	4.7	18	2
1984	16/15	432	279	3630	.646	80t	10	28	102.9	39	118	3.0	15	2
1985	15/15	494	303	3653	.613	66t	13	27	91.3	42	153	3.6	16	3
1986	8/8	307	191	2236	.622	48	9	8	80.7	17	38	2.2	17	0
1987	13/11	398	266	3054	.668	57t	13	31	102.1	35	141	4.0	20	1
1988	14/13	397	238	2981	.599	96t	10	18	87.9	38	132	3.5	15	3
1989	13/13	386	271	3521	.702	95t	8	26	112.4	49	227	4.6	19	3
Totals	151/124	4059	2593	31054	.638	96t	107	216	94.0	371	1405	3.8	21	19

POSTSEASON

		Passing								Rushing				
	G/S	ATT	COMP	YDS	PCT	LONG	INT	TD	NFL RATG	ATT	YDS	AVG	LONG	TD
1981	3/3	88	56	747	.636	58t	4	6	94.4	12	4	0.3	7	1
1983	2/2	79	45	548	.570	76	2	4	85.1	7	56	3.2	18	0
1984	3/3	108	67	873	.620	40	5	7	89.9	13	144	11.1	53	1
1985	1/1	47	26	296	.553	36	1	0	65.7	1	0	0.0	0	0
1986	1/1	15	8	98	.533	24	2	0	34.2	0	0	0.0	0	0
1987	1/1	26	12	109	.462	33	1	0	42.0	3	20	6.7	14	0
1988	3/3	90	56	823	.622	61t	1	8	117.0	11	39	3.5	11	0
1989	3/3	83	65	800	.783	72t	0	11	146.0	5	19	3.8	10	0
Totals	17/17	536	335	4294	.625	76	16	36	97.5	52	282	5.4	53	2

JERRY RICE

PRO STATISTICS

		Receiving					Rushing			
	G/S	NO.	YDS	AVG	LONG	TD	ATT	YDS	AVG	LONG	TD
1985	16/4	49	927	18.9	66t	3	6	26	4.3	15t	1
1986	16/15	86	1570	18.3	66t	15	10	72	7.2	18	1
1987	12/12	65	1078	16.6	57t	22	8	51	6.4	17	1
1988	16/16	64	1306	20.4	96t	9	13	107	8.2	29	1
1989	16/16	82	1483	18.1	68t	17	5	33	6.6	17	0
Totals	76/63	346	6364	18.3	96t	66	42	289	6.9	29	4

POSTSEASON

		Receiving					Rushing			
	G/S	NO.	YDS	AVG	LONG	TD	ATT	YDS	AVG	LONG	TD
1985	1/1	4	45	11.3	20	0	0	0	0.0	0	0
1986	1/1	3	48	16.0	24	0	0	0	0.0	0	0
1987	1/1	3	28	9.3	13	0	0	0	0.0	0	0
1988	3/3	21	409	19.4	61t	6	3	29	9.6	21	0
1989	3/3	19	317	16.7	72t	5	0	0	0.0	0	0
Totals	9/9	50	847	16.9	72t	11	3	29	9.6	21	0

JOE MONTANA—1990 RECORD SHEET

GAME	OPPONENT	SCORE	WIN OR LOSE	Passing							Rushing				
				COMP	ATT	PCT	YDS	INT	LONG	TD	ATT	YDS	AVG	LONG	TD
1															
2															
3															
4															
5															
6															
7															
8															
9															
10															
11															
12															
13															
14															
15															
16															
TOTALS															
PLAY-OFF GAME															
PLAY-OFF GAME															
PLAY-OFF GAME															
SUPER BOWL															
TOTALS															

JERRY RICE—1990 RECORD SHEET

GAME	OPPONENT	SCORE	WIN OR LOSE	Receiving					Rushing				
				RECEPT	YDS	AVG	TD	LONG	ATT	YDS	AVG	LONG	TD
1													
2													
3													
4													
5													
6													
7													
8													
9													
10													
11													
12													
13													
14													
15													
16													
TOTALS													
PLAY-OFF GAME													
PLAY-OFF GAME													
PLAY-OFF GAME													
SUPER BOWL													
TOTALS													

93

I hope that you liked this book. If you did,
you would probably like our other sports titles
by Richard J. Brenner:

Michael Jordan • Magic Johnson. A dual
biography of the two most popular athletes
in America. A look behind the scenes and
above the rim.

• Featuring 12 exciting photos.

The World Series: The Great Contests. The
unique excitement of the Fall Classic is brought
to life in seven of the most thrilling contests of
all time. From Jackie Robinson and the Brooklyn
Dodgers to Dave Stewart and the Oakland A's.

• Featuring 16 pages of action-packed photos.

The Complete Super Bowl Story Games I-XXIV.
The most exciting moments in Super Bowl history
are brought to life, game-by-game.

• Featuring 16 pages of action-packed photos.
• Record Sheets for Super Bowl XXV.

Order now! Send a check or money order for
$4.20 *per* book ($2.95 + $1.25 postage and
handling) to:

East End Publishing
54 Alexander Dr.
Syosset, NY 11791

Quantity discounts available for orders of 25 or more

Please send me _____ total copies as indicated:
JORDAN • JOHNSON ☐   THE WORLD SERIES ☐
    THE COMPLETE SUPERBOWL STORY ☐
I am enclosing $4.20 for each copy ordered. Send
books to:

Name_____

Address_____

City_____ State_____ Zip_____

Allow four weeks for delivery.